BOTTICELLI

ALBERTO BUSIGNANI

GROSSET & DUNLAP
Publishers - New York

First American edition published 1967 by Grosset & Dunlap, Inc.

Translated from the Italian by Edward Allen

Library of Congress Catalog Card Number: 67-24226

Printed and bound in Italy

Life

The available facts reveal very little about Botticelli: his paintings tell us most about his life, indeed they reflect the ideas and mood of the late Florentine Quattrocento better than any other contemporary work. Neo-Platonism and the preaching of Savonarola interacted to create a period of spiritual upheaval in his native town during his life. We will first consider the chronological facts, and leave aside the question of his relationship with the society of his time until we examine the theory of art which was the true expression of his personality. He was drawn by temperament to the contemplation of Beauty as an ideal, and as a result his nature found little expression in action: anecdotes, therefore, sometimes a useful guide to the personality of an artist, are extremely rare.

The main events of Botticelli's life are quickly stated. He was born in 1445; this information appears in a tax-return belonging to his father, who was a tanner, Mariano di Vanno Filipepi. Sandro was sent to school in 1458, as we know from another tax-return, in which his father says: 'Sandro, my son, aged thirteen, is at his books and in poor health.' A little later, according to Vasari, he began as an apprentice in the studio of Filippo Lippi (*c.* 1465), and remained there probably until 1467, the year in which Filippo established himself permanently in Spoleto. In the *Ricordanze* of Benedetto Dei we find that in 1470 Botticelli painted his work *Fortitude* (now in the Uffizi) for the Court of the Merchants (Mercatanzia). In 1474 he painted the *St Sebastian* (now in Berlin) for the church of Santa Maria Maggiore, and the same year left for Pisa, where he began a fresco, now lost, for the Cappella Incoronata of the cathedral.

From this time onwards nearly all the references to him concern the paintings: a standard painted for Giuliano de' Medici for an allegorical pageant set to music by Poliziano in 1475; in the year of the Pazzi plot, 1478, a series of portraits of the conspirators who were hanged near the

Palazzo Vecchio; and the *St Augustine* for the church of Ognissanti, in 1480.
In June 1481 Pope Sixtus IV summoned Botticelli, along with other principal painters from Umbria and Florence, to Rome to decorate the walls of the Sistine Chapel. He remained there until the spring, or possibly the autumn, of 1482. His father Mariano died in this year. There is also a record of a contract with the Florentine Signoria listing the names of Ghirlandaio, Perugino, Piero del Pollaiolo and Biagio d'Antonio Tucci, for the decoration of the Sala dei Gigli in Palazzo Vecchio. Only one of these frescoes was carried out: Ghirlandaio's *St Zenobius,* which is still extant. An altarpiece (now in Berlin) was painted in 1485 for the Bardi chapel in the church of Santo Spirito. The Uffizi *Annunciation* for the church of Cestello (now Santa Maria Maddalena dei Pazzi) dates from 1488-90, and in 1491 he was one of a panel of judges, with Baldovinetti, Ghirlandaio, Perugino and Lorenzo di Credi, at work on the commission for the façade of the cathedral of Santa Maria del Fiore.
Botticelli's brother Giovanni died in 1493. Giovanni was called *il Botticello* ('little cask'), from which it is generally assumed the painter's surname derived, though Vasari denies it. In 1496 he received a letter of introduction from Michelangelo in Rome to Lorenzo di Pier Franco dei Medici, in whose Villa at Castello he executed various decorations the following year. In 1499 we have the only reference which links his name with that of Savonarola; on 2 November his brother Simone Filipepi wrote in his journal: 'My brother Alessandro di Mariano Filipepi, one of the best painters we have in our city, was seated in my house by the fire at three o'clock one night. He told me he had spoken about Fra' Girolamo (Savonarola) with Doffo Spini in his workshop that day. Knowing that Doffo had acted as a principal during the interrogation of the friar, Sandro questioned him and asked him to tell the whole truth. He wished to know what sins they had found in Fra' Girolamo, which caused them to condemn him to that dreadful death. Sandro said: "Why did you condemn him?" He replied: "I did not condemn him, our leader was responsible,

Benozzo Federighi. If we had let him return to San Marco with his friends, the population would have pillaged our goods and torn us to pieces. Things had gone so far we had to put him to death to save our own lives." The bluntness of this report and the single wary question put by Botticelli can leave little doubt as to his reformist sympathies. The anguished and prophetic style of the final paintings seems further to support this view.

Nearing the end of his life, in 1501, Botticelli painted the *Mystic Nativity* which is now in London. He planned, through his contacts with Annabella Gonzaga's agent in 1502, to complete the decoration of Isabella's Studiolo, begun by Mantegna. Botticelli's popularity as an artist had by this time declined. This commission, which he would gladly have accepted, had already been rejected by Perugino and Filippo Lippi. In 1504 he was a member of the commission set up to decide on the final location for Michelangelo's *David.* He died in 1510. His name was entered in the *Libro dei Morti* (book of the dead) of the city of Florence and that of the Physicians and Apothecaries' Guild, to which he had belonged since 1499. His remains were buried on 7 May in the cemetery of the church of Ognissanti.

To complete this brief account of Botticelli's life, it is worth turning to Vasari's *Lives,* that great panorama of Italian artistic civilization, for a judgment by a near-contemporary on Botticelli's status as a painter. The reference to Botticelli is perfunctory and inadequate; but this is not the place to attempt an assessment of Vasari's true qualities as a critic and as a biographer.

Vasari begins: 'In the time of the illustrious Lorenzo de' Medici the elder, which was truly an age of gold for men of talent, there flourished a certain Alessandro, called after our custom Sandro, and further named Di Botticello, for a reason which we shall presently see. His father, Mariano Filipepi, a Florentine citizen, brought him up with care, and caused him to be instructed in all such things as are usually taught to children before they choose a calling. But although the boy readily mastered whatever he wished to learn, he was constantly discontented; neither would he take any pleasure in reading, writing or reckoning, so that the father, exasperated by his son's waywardness [the choice of words is a typical piece of Vasarian intolerance], apprenticed him in despair to a friend of his named Botticello, a goldsmith who was an able master of his craft. There was at that time a close and constant intercourse between the goldsmiths and the painters, and Sandro, who possessed considerable ingenuity, and was strongly disposed to the arts of design, became enamoured of painting and resolved to devote himself entirely to that vocation.'

There is no evidence of an apprenticeship to any goldsmith of that name in Florence; it is therefore more likely that Botticelli's name came from his brother Giovanni.

'He acknowledged his purpose at once to his father, and the latter, who knew the force of his inclinations, took him accordingly to the Carmelite monk, Fra' Filippo, who was a most excellent painter of that time, with whom he placed him to study the art, as Sandro himself had desired. Devoting himself thereupon entirely to the vocation he had chosen, Sandro so closely followed the directions and imitated the manner of his master, that Fra' Filippo conceived a great love for him, and instructed him so effectually, that Sandro rapidly attained to such a degree in art as none would have predicted for him.'

Apart from the reference on the first page to his apprenticeship with Lippi, the really important information which Vasari conveys here concerns Botticelli's restlessness and discontent as a student, and Vasari hints at it again later with his customary psychological penetration, referring to Botticelli as a *persona sofistica* (a refined and studious man). The dubious list of paintings given by Vasari can be ignored, as it is less important than the anecdotes, which, superficial as they are made to seem by the writer, give a better understanding of Botticelli's personality. If we turn for a moment to Vasari's life of Cosimo Rosselli, who was, with Botticelli, one of the painters who helped to decorate the Sistine Chapel, the reactions of Pope Sixtus IV to their work may help to bring to light Botticelli's discontent and basic unwillingness to adapt himself to the atmosphere in Rome: 'Cosimo sought to hide a deficiency of imagination and drawing by covering his work with the finest ultramarine and other bright colours. He embellished his picture with much gold; there were neither trees, grass, drapery nor cloud that was not touched with it. So he hoped to make the Pope, who was not very well versed in the art, believe that he merited the first prize. The day the paintings were to be unveiled, his was seen with the rest. Instead of taking pity on him, the other artists mocked and derided his work. But, in the end, they were the ones who were mocked, for those colours which Cosimo had invented so dazzled the eyes of the Holy Father, who understood very little about these things, that he reckoned Cosimo had done better than all the others. Thus, having given him the prize, he commanded that the others cover their works with the finest blue and gold that could be found, so that theirs would be equal in richness and colour to the paintings of Cosimo. So these wretched painters, in despair at having to satisfy the Pope's ignorance, set themselves to the task of undoing the good work they had done. As a result Cosimo was able to laugh at those who shortly before had made a fool of him.' Whether or not we believe in these grave consequences of the Holy Father's incomprehension, the worldly ostentation of Rome is expressed typically by Vasari's amused treatment of the subject. This was evidently an environment which was quite unacceptable to Botticelli's 'refined and studious' nature.

Returning to Vasari's life of Botticelli: 'Sandro was fond of joking, and often amused himself at the expense of his disciples and friends . . . A weaver of cloth once came to live close to Sandro, and this man erected eight looms, which, when all were at work, caused an intolerable din with the trampling of the weavers and the clang of the shuttles, so that poor Sandro was deafened with it, and produced such a trembling and shaking throughout the house, which was not too solidly built, that the painter could not continue his work or even remain in the house. He frequently requested his neighbour to put an end to his disturbance, but the latter replied that he would do what he pleased in his own house. Angered by this, Sandro had an enormous stone of great weight, more than would fill a waggon, placed in exact equilibrium on the wall of his own dwelling, which was higher than that of his neighbour, and not very strong; this stone threatened to fall at the slightest shake given to the wall, when it must have crushed the roof, floors, frames, and workmen of the weaver to atoms. Terrified, the man hastened to Sandro, who gave him his own reply in his own words, namely that he would do what he pleased in his own house; the weaver was compelled to come to reasonable terms, and to be a less troublesome neighbour.'

We find it further related, that Sandro Botticelli once, in jest, accused a friend of his own of heresy. When called before the judge, the accused naturally demanded to know by whom he was accused and of what. Being told that Sandro had declared him to hold the opinion of the Epicureans, that the soul dies with the body, he required that his accuser should be confronted with him before the judge. Sandro was summoned accordingly, and the accused man exclaimed: 'It is true that I hold the opinion stated respecting the soul of this man, who is a brute beast; is he not also a heretic, for without a grain of learning, scarcely knowing how to read, has he not undertaken to make a commentary on Dante, and take his name in vain?'

Both episodes are rather commonplace, though the final one is typical of the traditional tales of the period, from Sacchetti's *Novelle* to the tale of the Fat Woodcutter (*Il Grasso Legnaiolo*). And yet, viewed in the contest of Botticelli's last years, his sympathy with Savonarola and his sense of a tragic fate, the anecdotes acquire a deeper significance which was beyond Vasari's power to comprehend. The despair and affliction underlying these stories was ignored, and Vasari could only offer his usual sententious and basically unimaginative statement of the facts. 'This master is said to have had an extraordinary love for those whom he knew to be zealous students in art [here we have an example of Vasari's insight], and is affirmed to have earned considerable sums of money; but as he was a bad manager and very careless, all came to nothing. Finally, having become old, unfit for work, and helpless, he was obliged to go on crutches, being unable to stand upright, and so died, after long illness and decrepitude, in his seventy-eighth year.'

Works

Lippi, Pollaiolo and Verrocchio were the formative influences in the early years of Botticelli's career. This has been the view of modern criticism until recently. Verrocchio can be momentarily disregarded; his place in the early Quattrocento must remain doubtful until the corpus of his work has been more adequately studied. Both Pollaiolo and Lippi, however, are of immediate importance to our discussion: Pollaiolo was the last representative of the revolution in art during the early years of the fifteenth century; Lippi, with his acute faculty of perception, had investigated many of the problems that had survived from the amazing social and political revival which took place in Florence around 1460. Sandro's early association with these painters was not only an opportunity to develop formal inventiveness and enrich his style, it introduced him to the two great alternative systems of expression which were being developed from the study of Masaccio's art, the central theme of the century until the advent of Michelangelo.

Any reference to Sandro's development at this time involves the whole of the period around 1470, dominated by the aged Lippi, by Pollaiolo, still in the early stages of his maturity, and by the fledgling Leonardo; we can appreciate the importance of the Florentine absorption of early Renaissance influences. It should be remembered that in the preceding period both Masaccio and Brunelleschi based their beliefs on the autonomy of man (Giotto's view had been similar, as is now recognized by modern studies) and by implication accorded a similar autonomy to nature, implying hypothetically the existence of a natural reality which was a concrete and self-consistent value: nature was therefore, neither the exclusive domain of man's reason nor a manifestation of the divine will (the medieval 'daughter of God'). Brunelleschi in fact formulated perspective as a science of existence as well as vision: implying a concordance between man, who exists through his vision, and nature, which exists in the vision of man. The concept is clear enough, and is confirmed in Alberti's *Trattato della Pittura,* where these theoretical ideas were applied to colourful descriptions of complex landscapes for the instruction of artists. Some of these ideas are evident in certain landscape details of Masaccio's Carmine frescoes; they appear to prove the faultiness of certain widely held theories about the nature of early Renaissance art which place undue emphasis on man as the architect of his own fate, *faber fortunae suae* (of which Donatello's powerful figure of Gattamelata is considered an example), and consequently neglect the importance of the ideas of the early fathers of the Renaissance. This misunderstanding affects interpretations of Botticelli and his period: the so called 'heroic' influences of Brunelleschi, Donatello and Masaccio are emphasized to the detriment of the less obvious qualities which they share with, say, Domenico Veneziano. Again, Pollaiolo's 'Herculean' qualities have been emphasized, but his poetically rarified expression of nature has been largely ignored.

This critical view is understandable, since Florentine painters were obsessed with purely formal problems. Nevertheless, Domenico Veneziano's interpretation of Masaccio, in landscape particularly, was developed mainly outside Florence, by Piero della Francesca (one of the 'fathers' of the Renaissance, and, incidentally, of major importance to the landscape-based art of Venice). Domenico Veneziano, and his follower Alessio Baldovinetti, also influenced Antonio Pollaiolo, and the wider implications of Pollaiolo's art were later passed on to Leonardo. This development can clearly be traced back to Giotto, in whose work nature was incidental to the concept of man. In Masaccio, and even more in Domenico Veneziano, an equilibrium is maintained between human nature and the surrounding cosmos. Finally, in Pollaiolo, nature is the domain of Pan, while man is transformed into Hercules, and himself becomes a mythical creature. Leonardo, later in the century, developed the theme of man's position as an 'elemental' force of nature.

This line of development was also the most important for Botticelli between 1460-70, while Lippi's influence still survived as a contrary impulse. Lippi had elaborated his own elegant version of Masaccio's humanism, and of his interpreta-

tion of landscape; the *Madonna and Child with St John* in the Uffizi is the most transparently beautiful expression of this evolution of his style.
Lippi failed to understand the inner validity of Masaccio's perspective: space considered as an environment rationally organized by the action of man; reality made concrete and inalienable. Above all Masaccio had made perspective into a practical instrument with which to manipulate and collate his images. What Lippi did understand so well was the autonomous value of the human figure; he took advantage of his own spatial deficiencies, and concentrated on the plastic expression of his line, with the image tied to the plane of the picture. Landscape is pushed far back, almost as if seen through the wrong end of a telescope, and also tends to add to the isolation of the figures.
Of real importance here is the fact that Masaccio's and Brunelleschi's idea of man was once again in question. With the exclusion of a 'concrete' environment (present, however, in a narrative, descriptive way in Domenico Veneziano, and the austere geometric interiors of Andrea del Castagno) the image becomes symbolic and lyrically suggestive, and has no active or concrete reality.
The course open to Botticelli was a choice between two sets of ideas taken from a single source. Pollaiolo represented the intellectual naturalistic trend at its most refined. Lippi was basically a humanist, though there were fourteenth-century additions in his work: the sophisticated love poems of Guido (Cavalcanti) and even the allegorically complex *Divine Comedy* of Dante were used as sources for the introduction of transcendental concepts into his work. These currents of thought had another and deeper significance. They reflected a change, or decline, in the civic ideas which had been characteristic of the revolutionary early fourteenth century. The introduction to Alberti's *Trattato della Pittura* contains passages which theorize the new Romanism. The institutions of the present were considered to be as important as past achievements. Alberti in fact preferred the work of his friends to the antique masters; 'those dear friends of mine Nencio [Ghiberti], Luca and Masaccio', and above all 'Pippo the architect [Brunelleschi]'.

The *Apostles* and the *Prophets* of Masaccio and Donatello had a new significance in the role they accorded to man, and the emphasis placed on individual responsibility and self-determination, important political and public virtues. But private virtues, even the old courtly habits, were coming into favour again, a tendency which was associated in Florence with the rise of the Medici. Taste also declined: Cosimo the Elder chose the feeble sub-Gothic architect Michelozzo in place of Brunelleschi for the convent of San Marco and the Ca' Fagiolo, and, just after the turn of the century, Piero the Gouty employed the mediocre talent of Benozzo Gozzoli to celebrate the Medici name in the chapel of the Palazzo di Via Larga.

As courtly behaviour gradually became general in Florentine society, the reaction against the austerity of the old customs grew. Rich new private palaces were built; tournaments and fairs (these show clearly the Medici influence on the taste of the period) were paid for out of the money earned by the merchants.

This changing situation was most closely reflected in the visual arts, particularly the emblematic paintings of the period, as we can see from Pollaiolo's work: the silver cross made for the Baptistry in Florence, and the dancing, griffin- or falcon-like figures on the walls of the Villa Gallina are instances of these. Pisanello's *Eustachi* and the aristocratic *Magi* of Gentile da Fabriano had been replaced by these fiercely energetic figures placed against the blue and gold of the coat of arms of the Medici. Into his landscapes Pollaiolo introduces the antique figures of Hercules or Apollo, more dashing perhaps than the real-life Federigo degli Alberighi, but basically not very different from him in their attitudes. The enlightened Signoria of the Medici served in fact to further the social, political and cultural decline of Florence. Worldly elegance and intellectual refinement were encouraged in the place of individual and public virtue. An almost medieval state of affairs was re-established, though enriched by the extraordinary cultural experience of the early years of the century.

In drawing his stylistic conclusions from the artistic wealth of the previous era Botticelli was bound to feel the appeal of Lippi's lyrical individuality. Lippi's painting, in its allusion to an ideal, was in line with the neo-Platonism favoured by the Medici court. We have also seen that it retained and revived medieval characteristics which were in keeping with the courtly manners reintroduced into public life by the Medici.

Having summarized thus briefly the prevailing cultural climate, we can turn to Botticelli's early works; the *Fortitude* of the Mercatanzia, 1470 (*pl. 9*), and the *St Sebastian,* in Berlin (*pl. 15*), which was previously dated, from an ancient source, 1474, and thought to have been painted for the church of Santa Maria Maggiore. It is not surprising that some stylistic confusion is evident in these early works. A plastic, linear movement derived from Pollaiolo is introduced into the more congenial Lippesque themes. As for landscape, the full implications of Pollaiolo's style have not been understood, and so it retains a secondary, purely decorative function in Botticelli's work.

The immediate consequence of Botticelli's choice of models is a refusal to consider perspective as an aid to representation, or as a basis for architectonic structure. Furthermore it involves the rejection of the idea of the man-nature relationship, though in a more drastic way than had ever occurred to Lippi, who in any case lacked the ability to see the full implications of his own style. To quote Leonardo, who immediately understood Botticelli, 'Sandro, why do you place the third thing before the second?' and, 'To one who does not love landscape it seems a subject unworthy of study, as our Botticelli said.'

The opposition between Pollaiolo and Botticelli can now be considered. Pollaiolo's work was so rich in possibilities that it was perhaps the most fruitful source of inspiration for Michelangelo and the early mannerist painters of Florence. Botticelli's earliest influence was through his contact with Lippi, as a student; 'he was taken to Filippo . . . an excellent painter of that time, and taught there in the master's own style' (Vasari). The impact of Pollaiolo's work is felt later. During this first period Botticelli produced a number of works which are variations of Lippi's *Madonna* in the Uffizi: *Innocenti Madonna* (*pl. 1*), *Fesch*

Madonna (*pl. 2*), *Madonna della Loggia* in the Uffizi, the *Guidi Madonna* in the Louvre, and the *Madonna* of the Accademia (*pl. 3*), the *Madonna del Roseto* in the Louvre, the *Duveen Madonna* in New York, and the *Corsini Madonna* in Washington.

These works show signs of Lippi's influence both in their thematic treatment and in their development of line and colour; while their subject-matter shows traces of the influence of Andrea Verrocchio's studio, which Botticelli may possibly have frequented after leaving Lippi.

The contribution of Verrocchio's studio to the development of Florentine painting between 1460 and 1470 is a complex question. Briefly, the source of 'Verrocchian' influence seems to lie not in Verrocchio himself but in an unknown artist. This 'Pseudo-Verrocchio' painted a series of panels, including a *Pietà*, now lost, which was signed, through a curious error on the part of some old restorer, 'Ant. Pollaioli'; the tabernacle in the Via del Campanile; *The Three Archangels* in the Uffizi; the *St Monica* in the church of Santo Spirito; and two panels in the Accademia representing *St Monica* and *St Augustine.* The Pseudo-Verrocchio is also presumed to be responsible for the pre-Leonardo portions of the *Baptism* in the Uffizi, although Ragghianti maintains that these are at least partly the work of Botticelli.

According to Mesnil, *The Three Archangels* was painted not later than 1467, and in my opinion this picture constitutes the true point of contact between Botticelli and the Pseudo-Verrocchio. It presents characteristics which are fundamental to Botticelli's creative style at the time when it was painted: the enhanced linear rhythms of the figure of Gabriel are post-Lippi in style, and the non-perspectival character of the landscape, which is basically inspired by Pollaiolo, enables the figures to be placed in isolation and emphasized. The effect is of a set-piece in which Lippi's ideas have been deliberately used and then refined upon by Botticelli. He has managed to instil into his line a descriptive quality which the friar never possessed. This development from the simple Lippi motive is carried a step further in a group of works (the *Madonnas* now in London, Naples and

Strasbourg) in which the composition is articulated and connects the figures with increased effectiveness. In the *Madonna and Child with two Angels* (*pls. 4-5*) the figures are grouped in an enclosed garden, and in the background, emphasized by an arrangement of trees, there is a rhythmically stylized landscape.
However, the influence of Pollaiolo was of vital importance in the move towards linear purity. Previously he had shown a tendency, through Lippi, to model his forms stiffly and in a rather dry relief reminiscent of Verrocchio. His figures now began to lose their inherent weight and become more expressive. This tendency is contradicted, however, in certain works painted under Pollaiolo's influence before the *St Sebastian* in Berlin; the *Fortitude* (*pl. 9*) and the *Holofernes* and *Judith* diptych in the Uffizi (*pls. 13-14*). These two works have harshly-modelled forms which again show a rather academic approach to Verrocchio. Botticelli's reaction to the lingering influences of his early period resulted in a further step in his stylistic development. Themes begin to appear in the paintings which point to his later style. Movement is explored as an externally expressed linear quality differing entirely from the latent energy and movement in Pollaiolo. Apart from the *Madonna and Saints* in the Uffizi, probably painted for the convent of Santa Elisabetta delle Convertite (*pls. 10-12*), the complex compositions of other works have a metallic quality, and linear flexibility is only occasionally evident; although this particular linear character is predominant in the Hutton portrait and the one in the Pitti (*pl. 8*).
Considering Botticelli's work as a series of successive periods, it must be admitted that we meet with certain apparent inconsistencies of style. The relative complexity of composition is often the cause of stylistic confusion. In compositions which are basically architectonic, such as the *Madonna and Saints* (*pls. 10-12*), the artist still has difficulty in using line as a structural element. He finds it easier to introduce line into paintings of simple contruction and single forms, such as portraits where the figure is placed against an abstract background. His stylistic ideas now run counter to those of his former master Lippi. His works of this

period represent a stylistic compromise between Verrocchio and Pollaiolo, and already hint at an individual pictorial language of his own. We do not know whether he realized very clearly the implications of the work of Pollaiolo. At any rate he showed more interest in Pollaiolo's experimental, non-religious approach than in Lippi's humanism. Though he was probably unaware of it, Lippi's paintings did in fact hold possibilities for religious and mystical expression by means of allegories. In any case it is fairly obvious that his personal development at this time was dictated more by instinctive feeling than by any critical assessment of the stylistic influences around him. Intuition was of more use to him than speculation as a means of understanding the nature of ideal reality. In fact a continual refinement of intuition runs parallel to his development as a painter, and in this way he sensed the implications of both neo-Platonism and the later movement led by Savonarola. Formal problems of the early period were no longer a preoccupation to him. Before considering the *St Sebastian* in Berlin, which marks the peak of his maturity, we should examine the *Adoration of the Magi* in the National Gallery, London. The problems of documentation and of dating are considerable. The date suggested by Salvini (in his 'Note sul Botticelli', 1962) seems the most plausible; an earlier one would place it out of step with the line of development followed so far. Salvini claims four characteristics of note: 'awkward composition and timid execution, Lippi's influence especially in the upper portion, pointing to the early style of Botticelli, *c.* 1465; the presence of certain figures showing Pollaiolo's influence, belonging to Botticelli's style shortly after 1470; and, finally, parts by the hand of Filippino: it is known that Filippino was working in Botticelli's workshop in 1472. This painting was therefore planned and begun by Botticelli in Filippo Lippi's studio about 1465-66, and for this reason may be considered one of Botticelli's earliest works, painted immediately after the earlier variations on Lippi's famous *Madonna.* It was left unfinished and continued later by Botticelli with Filippino's help. His young pupil was given a free hand in the painting of heads and figures, though not permitted to interfere by correcting or over-painting. The date 1470 seems reliable, judging from the presence of Filippino (this pupil probably entered the studio some time before 1472), and from the more fully developed figures in the composition, which were painted entirely by Botticelli in the final phase of the work. These are definitely Pollaiolesque figures corresponding to the period of the so-called *Man with the Medal,* and the *Judith* diptych, which anticipates the *St Sebastian* of 1473-4.'

In style the *St Sebastian* can be more closely related to Pollaiolo than any other of Botticelli's paintings. It also shows the emergence of an individual pictorial language. The reciprocal influences of Botticelli and Pollaiolo are again present: line, however functional, accentuates the two-dimensional quality of the image, so that the figure is on the same plane as the background. The general effect is melodic and consists of a play of precise colour zones without emphasis on movement and space (*pl. 15*). Masaccio's contribution to art was being evolved by Pollaiolo into a new painting of nature in evolution; overt physical action replaces the action latent in Masaccio. Pollaiolo believed in *homo sive natura sive deus* (man=nature=god), and his art was built up on this concept; no doubt he hoped that his work might become the expression of a personal religion of nature. Historical developments in painting meant nothing to Botticelli: action was a quality to be transformed into contemplation, and myth the natural vehicle through which this could be achieved.

Like Botticelli, Lippi was unaffected by the historical implications of Masaccio's work. Lippi's art, among the trends and creative possibilities of the time, was only significant for the freedom and extravagance of its expression. The *Judith* diptych (*pls. 13-14*) is an example of a work in which, even prior to the *St Sebastian,* we can observe true Botticellian characteristics. This is a representation of the discovery of Holofernes' body and the pensive return of Judith to Betulia. Action is ignored, and everything is concentrated into a contemplation of the melancholy of the irrevocable.

If we now examine the mythical content of Botticelli's and Pollaiolo's works we shall notice that in the myth of

Pollaiolo time is natural, not historical; action is co-extensive with space. Hercules can therefore appear suddenly, like an essence of nature. With Botticelli there is no need for an illusion of space and action; there is simply time which is an ideal dimension. Moral truth and beauty, the individual and the cosmos are united – though much later his work changes and the subjects become identified with the tragic fate of the divinity.

There is a series of portraits, datable about the time of the *St Sebastian*, in which the single-figure-and-background theme is refined still further: the *Man with the Medal of Cosimo the Elder* (*pl. 16*), the *Profile Portrait of a Woman* (*pl. 18*), a modulation of lyrical line and muted colours, and the portraits of *Lorenzo* and *Giuliano de' Medici* (*pl. 17*). Slightly later (*c.* 1476) in the *Adoration of the Magi* (*pls. 19-23*), Pollaiolesque linear inflections are deliberately diminished. We should notice here that throughout these works space and perspective are progressively eliminated still further. Traditional perspective is still used in the *Convertite Madonna* (*pls. 10-12*), though in the *Adoration* tondo in the National Gallery, London (contemporary with the last stages of the other London *Adoration*), perspective and space are only a lyrical suggestion. In this tondo the setting which surrounds the figures is partly hidden by the spreading of the group in the central foreground. The classical ruins have become timelessly symbolic, typical therefore of Botticelli's classicism up until his last works. In the Uffizi *Adoration* there is a much greater effort towards linear consistency of style, rhythmically linking and binding the ruins and figures together; the effect is to turn the whole scene into an ideal allegory outside time. This is a strictly historical work, painted for the Medici family and intended as an exaltation of the artist's patrons, but the portrait figures of Cosimo, Giovanni, Lorenzo and Giuliano, and Botticelli himself, introduce a mood of absolute contemplation.

By the time of the Uffizi *Adoration,* and in particular the *Madonna of the Sea* in the Accademia, Florence (*pls. 24-5*), derivations of detail and structural form from Pollaiolo have been absorbed into a serene and confidently poetical style, in which he was able to express his concepts without effort. Next in chronological order is the *Spring* (*pls. 26-32*), one of Botticelli's greatest poetic achievements, in which he identifies himself completely with one of the main idealistic preoccupations of his work so far, Ficino's neo-Platonism.

Vasari's description of the subject is splendid although inadequate: '*Venus, accompanied by the Graces adorned with flowers, announcing Spring*'. However, it is similar to the suggestion put forward by Warburg; that the *Spring* represents the realm of Venus, inhabited by eternal spring, and he also believes that the idea is derived from Poliziano. It is impossible to cover all the hypotheses that have been put forward; the reader may, if he wishes, consult Salvini's thorough analysis (1962), which follows that of Gombrich (1945), who suggests that the painting is a celebration of the virtue of *humanitas,* taken from the philosopher Ficino. Gombrich also maintains that Poliziano's poetry is the link here between Ficino and Botticelli.

Salvini sums up: 'Poliziano is not Ficino; his poetry softens the harsh character of neo-Platonism; there is a sweet, fresh idyllic quality in it which is touched with a nostalgia for an antiquity which he admires (though not without a touch of subtle mockery) as the place where the senses and the spirit keep their eternal youth. This explains why, in Botticelli's representation of Venus as *humanitas* and spirit of universal love, the traditional meaning of Venus as the goddess of love and pleasure is not completely ignored. And also why, on the right hand side, the allegory begins with an allusion to the erotic myth of Flora and Zephyr, while on the left it concludes with the skyward-gazing figure of Mercury (signifying Reason and Knowledge). Venus, therefore, is *humanitas,* the virtue which comes from universal love (which Ficino considered the motive force of the world). This platonic love envelops and sublimates earthly love. Man's soul, according to Ficino, is divided through its double attraction both to God and to the body. "By a certain natural instinct it ascends to the heights and descends to the depths (*naturali quodam instinctu ascendit ad supera, discendit ad infera*)", and so even when attracted to the body the soul is linked with its essence, and therefore "free from moral reproof" (O. Kristeller: *Il pensiero filosofico di Marsilio Ficino,* Firenze, 1953). Venus then, like the human soul, is centrally placed, flanked by earthly love (Zephyr and Flora), the serene happiness of the Hour (Flora transformed into Venus by Spring), Beauty (the Graces between Delight and ambivalent Love), and the source of the intellectual contemplation of God (Mercury). Venus therefore incarnates the Platonic virtue of *humanitas* without discarding any of her attributes as the goddess of Love.' It may now be easy to see how Botticelli's contemplative non-historical form of art had developed at this point into a suitable instrument by which contemporary neo-Platonism might be interpreted. And also that his encounter with Ficino and Poliziano had been a logical consequence of tendencies reaching far back in time. From a strictly formal point of view the *Spring* is the final confirmation of the type of pictorial organization noted in his works so far. Space is eliminated and nature is dematerialized into Idea. A linear rhythm running through the whole image is brought into the foreground, and the modulation of colour is carefully balanced. Contemporary with this supreme poetic achievement we have the *St Augustine* in the church of Ognissanti (*pl. 33*), dated aproximately 1480, in which Botticelli reintroduces the traditional theme of a solidly constructed architectural perspective. A heaviness and angularity in the anatomy, characteristic of the plastic style of Andrea del Castagno, suggests that Sandro might have been interested in Castagno's work since 1478, at which time he was commissioned to paint, on the side of the Palazzo Vecchio, the Pazzi conspirators who had been hanged after the unsuccessful plot which had resulted in the death of Giuliano de' Medici. Botticelli may have been impressed by similar figures of the Albizi in the fresco by Andrea del Castagno on the Bargello, but it seems unlikely that he could have been influenced by a style so out of keeping with his own. And in fact, in the *St Augustine* we see that the cramped architectural surrounding has the effect of eliminating space *ab initio,* the saint's legs have no possibility of being in full perspective, and the cornice above appears to be cut short at one end. Line and colour superimposition, rather than chiaroscuro, is used to give plasticity. A preferable source for this work is perhaps the *St Jerome with a headless female saint* in the church of St Domenico di Pistoia, attributed variously to Pollaiolo and Verrocchio, but which, in the author's opinion, probably comes from the studio of the Pseudo-Verrocchio mentioned previously. This interpretation is further supported by the *Annunciation of San Martino alla Scala* (*pls. 34-5*), painted in 1485, a year later than the *St Augustine*. Here again the perspective is compressed in the foreground of the painting, and the distant landscape behind has no connection with any vanishing point. The linear contorsions in the figures have increased, bringing to mind the late period, in which serene and tragic elements, as well as allegorically sacred and profane subjects, alternate and conflict. We can however see in the figure of the angel which descends softly from above, and in the rhythmic curve of the Virgin as she bends modestly forward, something of the crystalline purity of *Spring*. Perhaps it would not be too fanciful to sense in these contrasts the first hints of an approaching storm.

Botticelli was in Rome between June 1471 and September 1482. He was summoned there by Pope Sixtus IV to decorate the walls of the Sistine Chapel, with Ghirlandaio, Cosimo Rosselli and Perugino (later joined by Signorelli, Pinturicchio and Piero di Cosimo). This can be thought of as a break in Botticelli's career. He painted three frescoes of a narrative cycle, depicting scenes from the Old and New Testaments: *The Trials of Moses, The Temptation of Christ* (*pls. 37-9*) and *The Punishment of the Rebel Angels*. The requirements on Botticelli in Rome were hardly suited to his spiritual disposition: the frescoes were expected to be monumental and naturalistic in execution, and appropriate therefore to the contemporary environment of Rome. In effect, they were allegories of narrative type, in a naturalistic treatment, and, as such, required a creative approach totally different to that which produced the *Spring*, where allegory is the result of a process of abstraction without historical references of any kind. The Roman frescoes were intended to be realistically suggestive of space, action and

historical fact, and in consequence Sandro was only able to express individuality in a few details, such as the *Daughter of Jethro* in the *Trials of Moses,* and the *Girl carrying Wood* in the *Temptation of Christ.*
It has been suggested that Botticelli's first encounter with the ruins of ancient Rome, and therefore with the world of antiquity, was a decisive factor in his future development. This is hardly likely. It seems more probable that the artist found Roman remains depressingly solemn rather than monumental and impressive. The head of the Uffizi *Centaur* (although a common bas-relief motif in Roman sarcophagi) is really derived from the solid and colourful plastic values of Antonio and Piero del Pollaiolo, as exemplified in the three *Saints* by these artists in the church of San Miniato, the *Virtues* in the Mercatanzia, and the London *St Sebastian,* works in which Antonio's obsession with human anatomy is replaced by a more freely relaxed manner. The frescoes for the Villa Tornabuoni-Lemmi, which are now in the Louvre, were probably executed shortly after Botticelli's return from Rome, and are additional proof that the artist's experience in Rome was of little importance to his stylistic formation. The subjects portrayed are Lorenzo Tornabuoni standing in front of a group of figures symbolizing the Liberal Arts (*pl. 42*), and Venus who is offering gifts to a young girl (*pls. 43-5*). The line is fluent and melodic, flowing through the figures grouped in a space which is without depth, while the setting as a whole has no particular reference to a specific historical time. Here we can see that the painter has gladly returned to a conception of allegory, sublimating beauty and idea, which was entirely natural to him. On closer inspection a growing sadness of mood is evident in these works, particularly in the *Pallas.* This tendency was already latent in the Berlin *St Sebastian,* possibly accounting for the rather harsh stylistic treatment of this work, and results in a further loss of the equilibrium which had been so wonderfully captured in the *Spring.* The spiritual style of the period to which the *Spring* belongs is revived and taken a step further in a last group of works which are among the most delightful of Botticelli's entire production: the *Madonna of the Magnificat,* Uffizi (*pls. 48-*

9), the *Madonna and Child,* Museo Poldi Pezzoli, Milan (*pls. 50-1*), the *Venus and Mars,* National Gallery, London (*pl. 52*), and lastly the *Birth of Venus* (*pls. 53-5*). All these are new allegorical variations which reinterpret and elaborate the poetic concepts of neo-Platonism.

The force of Botticelli's rarefied 'secular' idealism was in no way attenuated by its further exploitation in these works, all of which belong to the period between 1482-85. In them Botticelli's neo-Platonism was dialectically reinforced by the introduction of a new vein of religious feeling. The neo-Platonic idealism of his former period was intensified to the point of identifying Idea with Divinity. The ideal and the real world are reconciled in the concept of Redemption. Allegory succeeds in transforming the world of reality; it does this by seeking the divine in man, a state typified in the serene equilibrium inherent in the identification of Virtue with Beauty, a point where all activity ceases, which in consequence constitutes a revelation of God and his work. Early Renaissance thought had been entirely different in its approach, seeking the link between God, man and nature in man's reason, and his active life. Botticelli, proceeding from Filippo Lippi's humanism, moves into the realm of the divine and the Idea; in the dialogue between God and Man which is the theme of the Redemption he finds the theme of his last period. Botticelli's approach has been called medieval, but in fact medieval transcendentalism is replaced in his thought by the idea of reason as the source of divine knowledge. His work remains, side by side with the experimentalism of Leonardo da Vinci, one of the essential achievements of the Renaissance – and this is confirmed by the fact that many of the stylistic and conceptual innovations of the 'divine' Michelangelo can ultimately be traced back to Botticelli.

The philosophical sadness which we saw in the *Pallas* is predominant in all the paintings of this period, 1482-85.

As the Idea becomes purer, man finds himself further from Elysium. In the *Madonna of the Magnificat* (*pls. 48-9*) this ultimate, pellucid perfection is symbolized in a circular composition. The abstract quality of the work is expressed perfectly in its elusive linear rhythms. The approachable

Virgins of Lippi have given way to a cold personification of abstract Love, a Platonic footnote to the Canticles.

The allegory of *Venus and Mars* (*pl. 52*) is perhaps an interpretation of Botticelli's own private world. Mars is lying inert on the ground, head thrown back as if overcome by the idea of Beauty. Venus lies near, but she is abstract, an unapproachable absolute being in a timeless world. This sense of absolute being is perfectly expressed in the *Birth of Venus,* which in its poetic intensity surpasses anything imagined by Poliziano. The nature of this work recalls the hypothesis concerning the soul in the philosophy of Ficino: the soul is suspended between *supera* and *infera* (the heights and the depths), between intelligence (concomitant with faith) and the material world. Here, I think, Argan's words are appropriate: 'This beautiful female form, with its diaphanous shapes and pure outlines, constitutes a rejection or a sublimation of its physical aspect. It is like a challenge on the part of the intellect – a challenge thrown in the face of sensuality.' Or we might say that by sublimation in Idea, matter and being are converted into intellect. We are now able to appreciate the relationship between Botticelli and Pollaiolo, and on a different level Leonardo. The opposition is basically that between idealism and empiricism. For Leonardo and Pollaiolo divinity is latent in matter, eluding its transcendence through action; for Botticelli matter is transfigured into intellect and contemplation, and finally Idea (*pls. 53-5*).

In the *Santo Spirito Altarpiece,* painted in 1485, now in Berlin, non-Christian, neo-Platonic subjects have been replaced by Christian themes. Tragic and anguished feelings become more evident. The style is agitated, so that the rhythmic perfection achieved in the *Venus* is destroyed. It seems as if the long-prepared crisis has finally erupted into both style and subject. The two worn and emaciated Saints on either side of the slender figure of the Virgin seem to oppress the infant Christ, and stand as symbols, at the same time, of the Annunciation and the Apocalypse. St John the Baptist and St John the Evangelist are allegorical symbols of the Redemption, and also prefigure the coming end of the world. Here the line is tense and burdened with *angst.*

Slightly later in date, the *Madonna of the Pomegranate* (*pls. 56-7*) can be considered a further variation on the theme of the *Magnificat*. The supremely poised beauty of the Madonna has a languor which comes close to expressing despair. This work is the lyrical expression of Botticelli's anguished maturity, though in his struggle for intense emotional effect the abstract, almost frigid, ideal perfection of previous works is somehow lost.

The *San Barnaba Altarpiece* (*pls. 58-9*), painted perhaps soon after the *Madonna of the Pomegranate,* follows the *Santo Spirito Altarpiece* in style. Its striking characteristic is again the ascetic emaciation and forlornness of the Saints (St John staring sadly out in an attitude of bewilderment). The sorrowful tension has had the effect of hardening the formerly rhythmic line, and brings to mind something of the preoccupations of the mannerist painters of a later period. But perhaps the architecture is the most significant, for decorative elements taken from natural forms are eliminated, and it thus departs from anything seen previously in Botticelli's work. In the *Santo Spirito Altarpiece* embellishments of this sort had still been used: three small niches, which emphasized its triptychal form, each containing a small decorative shrub. Here we have only a sumptuous apse, a heroic rostrum on which the Holy Mother and Child are raised above the faithful. This triumphal architecture represents an important moment of transition, Botticelli's final rejection of his concern for the sublimation of natural beauty, via the intellect. It stands as the painter's release from a vow; after it he joined the band of ' weepers ' who followed Savonarola.

His attraction to Savonarola was no doubt as spontaneous as the one he had previously conceived for neo-Platonism and Ficino. In other words, it is more likely that he voluntarily joined Savonarola's group of followers than that the friar's preaching merely influenced him. It may well have seemed an answer to many of the doubts which had preoccupied him since 1485. It is reasonable to assume that Sandro found a relief in Savonarola's sermons, from the formal and conceptual problems involved in the creation of previous paintings such as the *San Barnaba Altarpiece*. Certainly, the

connection with Savonarola was the source of the bare undecorated style of his last works: the *Annunciation* in the Uffizi (*pls. 60-1*), the *Lehman Annunciation* (*pl. 63*), the *St Augustine in his Cell* (*pl. 64*), the *Lamentations* in Munich (*pl. 66*) and Milan (*pl. 67*), the *Calumny* (*pls. 70-2*), the *Stories of Lucretia and Virginia* (*pl. 73*), the *Mystic Nativity* in London (*pl. 74*), and the *Crucifixion* in the Fogg Art Museum, Cambridge, Mass.
These works of Botticelli's last period form a progression from the theme of communion with the Deity (*St Augustine in his Cell*) to that of sacred drama (the *Mystic Nativity*) in which man is reduced to the role of an agonized spectator, able only to contemplate and pray. Hence the sense of desolation and helplessness in some of the individual figures in these compositions: the figures around Christ in the *Lamentation* scenes in the Milan and Munich paintings (*pls. 66-7*), the angels who sense an impending tragedy and embrace in the foreground of the *Nativity,* and the Magdalen who clutches the cross in the strange allegorical *Crucifixion* in the Fogg Art Museum.
Calumny (*pls. 70-2*) differs in some respects from the works just mentioned. Its story is the well-known one told by Lucian, of Apelles, the young man who was dragged by Calumny into the presence of Penitence and Truth. The story alludes to the impotence of man in the sight of evil. He is again a spectator. Argan, referring to the central group which includes the figure of Calumny, interprets the ceaseless movement as an allusion to eternal repetition, and suggests that the ornate hall in which the scene takes place is symbolic of 'a distant region containing the deep motives for man's action and the source of his ideas.' *Calumny* depicts man as a creature with intellect and feeling, but lacking Grace. He is also powerless. Without Redemption, he is powerless to achieve Justice.
In the last period allegory was still Botticelli's authentic spiritual mode of expression, as it had been throughout his career. Not surprisingly, at this time, from about 1490, he turned also to illustrations, commissioned by Lorenzo di Pierfranco, interpreting the *Commedia* of Dante. The historical importance of these allegories should not be overlooked;

for one thing their tormented lyricism and sensitive introspection were to become a source of inspiration to Florentine artists during the early mannerist period.

It is sad to think that at the end of Botticelli's life his fellow-citizens turned their backs on him, preferring the work of younger men, even products of his own studio such as Filippino. The Florentine agent of that arch-intellectual Isabella Gonzaga reported to his mistress that 'Allessandro Botechiella' was the only painter not burdened with commissions, and that he would 'gladly work for her.'

Botticelli and the Critics

In the brief review of Botticelli's life at the front of this book I suggested that, owing to his inability to respond to the painter's personality, Vasari failed him as a critic. We can imagine that Vasari was in some ways indifferent to Botticelli's work, which must have seemed archaic to him, and in its late period positively 'Gothic'. Certainly his painting did not fit in with the cultural interests of Vasari's own age. As has been suggested, the formal linear elements of Botticelli's art, and, on a deeper level, his anti-classical spirit, may have exercised an influence on the emergent personality of Michelangelo and on mannerism. In fact, this influence can be considered one of the vital links between the cultures of the Quattrocento and the Cinquecento, as meaningful as the connection between Pollaiolo's approach to landscape and Leonardo's investigations into the nature of natural phenomena. Of course, modern art history takes a wider view than Vasari, who shared the view of his time, in believing that all art was a continual evolution 'from Greek (Byzantine) to Latin (Roman)', from Giotto to the classicism of Michelangelo. The reaction against Botticelli in his own lifetime is perhaps understandable in the light of developments current in the early years of the sixteenth century, Botticelli's last active period; Leonardo and Michelangelo had already executed the *Cascina* and *Anghiari Cartoons,* which were introducing painters to new pictorial ideas.

The neglect of Botticelli persisted without interruption (even Lanzi's favourable criticism failed to stimulate interest in the painter), until his revival by the Pre-Raphaelites in the second half of the nineteenth century. Their appreciation of Botticelli, like that of other aesthetes of the period, was limited to the formal refinements of his style, and ignored the significance of the work as an expression of ideas. In fact Botticelli was normally, and very inappropriately, considered a primitive, except by Ruskin, who sensed the deep moral content pervading his work.

The immense volume of contemporary criticism of his work begins with Berenson, who examined the value of line and movement as they occurred in the paintings and the relation of the work to the whole Quattrocento period. Subsequent studies of value include: H. Ulmann, *Sandro Botticelli* (Munich 1893), the first fully-documented account of Botticelli's career; H. Horne, *Alessandro Filipepi Commonly Called Sandro Botticelli* (London 1908); W. Bode, *Botticelli* (Berlin 1921) and *Botticelli* (Stuttgart 1926); Schmarsow, *Sandro del Botticello* (Dresden 1923); Y. Yashiro, *Sandro Botticelli* (London 1925); A. Venturi, *Botticelli* (Rome 1925); G. Gamba, *Botticelli* (London 1937 and London 1947); S. Bettini, *Botticelli* (Bergamo 1924 and 1947); H. E. Gombrich, 'Botticelli's Mythologies' in *Journal of the Warburg and Courtauld Institutes* (London 1945); G. C. Argan, *Botticelli* (Geneva 1957); R. Salvini, *Botticelli* (Milan 1958), and 'Note sul Botticelli' and 'Interpretazioni politiche e interpretazioni filosofiche di alcune allegorie botticelliane', both in *Scritti di storia dell'arte in onore di Mario Salmi* (Rome 1962).

Notes on the Plates

1 Madonna and Child with an Angel. Panel, 60 × 87 cm. Florence, Ospedale degli Innocenti, Pinacoteca. Formerly attributed by Cavalcaselle to Lippi, then to Botticelli by Ulmann, and later also by Bode, Gamba, Berenson, and Salvini. Doubtful are: Van Marle and Bettini. Opposed are: Venturi and Mesnil.

2 Madonna and Child with an Angel. Panel, 70×110 cm. Ajaccio, Musée Fesch. Attributed to Botticelli by Berenson. Like all other works of 1465-70, this panel shows the influence of Lippi.

3 Madonna and Child with Young St John and Two Angels. Panel, 62 × 85 cm. Florence, Galleria dell'Accademia. Originally in Santa Maria Nuova, then in the Uffizi, and in 1919 removed to the Accademia. First ascribed to Botticelli by Bode, then by Ulmann, Schmarsow, Van Marle, Gamba, Berenson, Procacci, and Salvini. Ascribed by Horne and Venturi to the 'school of Botticelli'.

4 Madonna and Child with Two Angels. Panel, 71×100 cm. Naples, Galleria Nazionale di Capodimonte. The original attribution is by Bode, accepted by the majority of critics (Schmarsow, Yashiro, Gamba, Berenson, L. Venturi, Mesnil, Bettini, Davies, and Salvini), rejected by Horne.

5 Madonna and Child with Two Angels. Detail.

6 Madonna and Child with Cherubim. Panel, 65×120 cm. Florence, Uffizi. Bode's ascription to Botticelli is favoured by the majority of critics. Stylistically in the manner of Lippi and Verrocchio, with lyrical overtones and a developing linear technique.

7 Madonna and Child against a Rose Hedge. Panel, 64 × 124 cm. Florence, Uffizi. Bode ascribes this panel to Botticelli, and suggests a date slightly before 1470. His opinion is shared by most critics.

8 Portrait of a Young Man. Panel. Florence, Pitti. Traditionally ascribed to Andrea del Castagno (accepted by Cavalcaselle and Morelli), then to Piero di Cosimo by Schmarsow. The inclusion of the painting in Venturi's Botticelli list was accepted by Bode. Later Venturi attributed it to the school of Filippo Lippi. Botticelli's authorship is not accepted by Ulmann; Kühnel ascribes it to Botticelli, Van Marle to 'a friend of Sandro's', and Berenson to Ghirlandaio's workshop. Berenson later acknowledged its authenticity. Modern criticism agrees unanimously on Botticelli and dates the work around 1470.

9 Fortitude. Panel, 87×167 cm. Florence, Uffizi. This panel belongs to a series of seven Virtues intended as decorations for the backs of seats, or an ornamental wainscoting, in the Court of the Mercatanzia. Piero del Pollaiolo had already completed a figure of Charity for the same guild in 1469, probably in competition with Verrocchio, and afterwards was given the full commission. In May 1470 Tommaso Soderini, Botticelli's patron and close friend of Lorenzo il Magnifico, succeded in obtaining for him a commission for two more virtues, for one of which, the *Fortitude*, Sandro received payment in August of the same year. Eventually the second of these two virtues was again given to Piero. The whole series is now on view in one room in the Uffizi. A firm dating for the *Fortitude* is a determinant factor in any analysis of Botticelli's early style. The influence of Pollaiolo is predominant, as would be expected, and the context of style is Verrocchio. We agree with Salvini who considers Lippi, Verrocchio and Pollaiolo the artists who had a continuing influence on Botticelli's style. This view is also held by Yashiro, Bettini and Argan.

10 Madonna and Child with Saints. Panel; 194 × 170 cm. Florence, Uffizi. Formerly in the church of Sant'Ambrogio all'Accademia, could be identified as the panel painted by Botticelli for the Augustinian nuns of Santa Maria delle Convertite (mentioned by Antonio Billi, an anonymous critic of Gaddi, Vasari and Borghini). It was attributed to Andrea del Castagno by Cavalcaselle though later critics have all affirmed Botticelli's authorship and dated it about 1470.

11 Madonna and Child with Saints. Detail: the head of the Virgin.

12 Madonna and Child with Saints. Detail: St Catherine.

13 Holofernes found Dead. Panel, 25×31 cm. Florence, Uffizi. A small diptych panel, the companion piece being the *Judith* (*pl. 14*). It was presented to Bianca Cappello by Rodolfo Sirigatti (mentioned by Borghini), and inherited by her son, Don Antonio de' Medici. On the latter's death it went to the Uffizi. Its attribution to Botticelli by Borghini is unanimously accepted, though disagreement exists as to its dating, generally accepted as slightly after 1470, except by Yashiro and Bettini, who prefer slightly before 1470.

14 Judith. Panel, 24×31 cm. Florence, Uffizi.

15 St Sebastian. Panel, 75×195 cm. Berlin, Staatliche Museen. Attributed to Botticelli by Cavalcaselle. It is almost certainly the work described by the anonymous critic previously mentioned as being in Santa Maria Maggiore ('a panel of St Sebastian against a column, which was painted in January 1473'). The date is consonant with its Pollaiolesque style.

16 Portrait of a Man with the Medal of Cosimo the Elder. Panel, 44×57.5 cm. Florence, Uffizi. The attribution to Botticelli is by Morelli and universally accepted, except by Bode. Efforts have been made to identify the subject of this portrait with various members of the Medici family; Piero the Gouty, Giovanni di Cosimo and Piero di Lorenzo have been suggested at various times, but all these identifications seem unacceptable on chronological grounds. The date for the work is a matter of controversy, but we are inclined to accept Salvini's, which is *c.* 1473-4.

17 Portrait of Giuliano de' Medici. Panel, 36 × 54 cm. Bergamo, Accademia Carrara. There are three other versions of this portrait: in the Crespi collection, Milan, the Staatliche Museen, and the Kress Foundation, National Gallery, Washington. The prototype of the four remains doubtful: in our view it is perhaps the Crespi portrait which in relation to the other three has the figure in reverse, matching with the portrait of Lorenzo now in the Lazzaroni collection in Paris. The authorities for the attribution of the four portraits to Botticelli are as follows: for the one at Bergamo, Morelli, Ulmann and Berenson; Berlin, Bode, Van Marle, Yashiro; Milan, L. and A. Venturi, Valentiner, Gamba, Mesnil, Berenson and Salvini; Washington, Suida and Bettini.

18 Profile Portrait of a Woman. Panel, 40 × 61 cm. Florence, Pitti. Both attribution and subject of this painting are controversial. The traditional ascription to Botticelli is contested by Milanesi, Morelli, Berenson and Yashiro, and favoured by Bode, Schmarsow, A. Venturi, Van Marle, Gamba, L. Venturi, Mesnil, Bettini, Ciaranfi and Salvini. It is dated by Salvini in the Pollaiolesque period, c. 1475.

19 Medici Adoration of the Magi. Detail: portrait of Lorenzo il Magnifico (see *pl. 21*).

20 Medici Adoration of the Magi. Detail: portrait of Giuliano de' Medici (see *pl. 21*).

21 Medici Adoration of the Magi. Panel, 134×111 cm. Florence, Uffizi. The original attribution, now fully acknowledged, is from an ancient source which also gives the picture's location as Santa Maria Novella. The identification of the models is doubtful; the most likely interpretations are: the first king kneeling in front of the Virgin, Cosimo the Elder, the second and third, Piero the Gouty and Giovanni di Cosimo; the youth with the sword on the far left, Lorenzo the Magnificent; the man in a yellow cape on the far right is thought to be Botticelli. Ulmann sees a portrait of Lorenzo Tornabuoni in the young man wearing a feathered hat standing behind Botticelli; Filippo Strozzi in the old man standing by the right hand wall, and Agnolo Poliziano in the youth leaning on the shoulder of Lorenzo the Magnificent. The painting can be dated about 1477.

22 Medici Adoration of the Magi. Detail: the peacock.

23 Medici Adoration of the Magi. Detail: Botticelli's self-portrait.

24 Madonna of the Sea. Panel, 28.5 × 40.5 cm. Florence, Uffizi. Formerly in the convent of Santa Felicità. Gamba's ascription to Botticelli is accepted by Procacci and Salvini; while Boeck, Berti and Baldini think it is by Filippino Lippi.

25 Madonna of the Sea. Detail: the head of the Virgin.

26 Spring. Detail: the three Graces (see *pl. 28*).

27 Spring. Detail: the three Graces (see *pl. 28*).

28 Spring. Panel, 314×203 cm. Florence, Uffizi. The work was executed for Lorenzo di Pierfrancesco and is mentioned in ancient sources as being in the Villa di Castello, which Pierfrancesco bought in 1477 (Horne). After Lorenzo's death the panel passed to Giovanni delle Bande Nere, and later to his son, Cosimo I. It is referred to as in the latter's possession by Vasari. It was moved into the Uffizi from Villa di Castello in 1815, then to the Accademia, and back to the Uffizi in 1919. The best interpretation of this allegory is undoubtedly Warburg's. This is a representation of the realm of Venus based on an idea of Poliziano's; on the right Zephyr pursues and holds Flora, Flora is transformed by Zephyr into the Hour of Spring, while Venus stands in the middle, with the three Graces and Mercury on her right. Other interpreters have seen in it an allegory of Simonetta's death and her rebirth in Elysium (Jacobsen); the marriage of a poet, in the person of Mercury, with a female satyr (Wickhoff), and Venus appearing at the judgment of Paris, as described by Apuleius (Gombrich). The interpretation by Battisti is interesting; a representation of the seasons, with the various months from February (Zephyr) to September (Mercury).

29 Spring. Detail: Venus.

30 Spring. Detail: The Hour of Spring.

31 Spring. Detail: Flora.

32 Spring. Detail: Zephyr and Flora.

33 St Augustine in his Cell. Fresco, 112 × 152 cm. Florence, church of Ognissanti. Mentioned in ancient sources, particularly the Anonimo Gaddiano, who states that it was painted at the same time as Ghirlandaio's *St Jerome* (dated 1480). The date for this fresco is stylistically confirmed. Many experts have seen influences of Castagno in it.

34 Annunciation of San Martino alla Scala. Detached fresco, 550 × 243 cm. Florence, Belvedere, Mostra degli affreschi. Detail of the angel. This fresco originally decorated the loggia of the hospital of San Martino alla Scala, which later became the entrance hall of the church of the same name. The fresco was detached about 1920. Poggi's research gives further evidence to support the view that this work was painted by Sandro between April and May 1481, shortly before he went to Rome.

35 Annunciation of San Martino alla Scala. Detail: the Virgin.

36 Madonna Adoring the Child with Infant St John. Panel, tondo, diameter 95 cm. Piacenza, Museo Civico. It is not accepted as an entirely authentic work by the majority of critics (exceptions are Gamba and Mesnil). I support the suggestion that it was painted in collaboration about 1481.

37 Temptation of Christ. Fresco, 115 × 345.5 cm. Rome, Sistine Chapel. Landscape detail. The decoration '*affresco*' of the Sistine Chapel was assigned to Botticelli, Ghirlandaio, Perugino and Cosimo Rosselli by Pope Sixtus IV in 1481. It is assumed that by 27 October of that year (document published by Gnoli) each painter had completed one fresco, as the full payment for the commission was to be assessed on the work executed by that date. Ten stories from the Old Testament had still to be painted for the completion of the cycle by 15 March 1482. As the number of frescoes required had been increased, three more painters were brought in to help with the work, Pinturicchio, Signorelli and Piero di Cosimo. The subject of this series of frescoes is taken from parallel stories from the Old and New Testament.

38 Temptation of Christ. Detail: group of onlookers. The ecclesiastic facing outwards is thought to be either Raffaello Riario or Giuliano della Rovere, both nephews of the Pope.

39 Temptation of Christ. Detail: the girl carrying wood.

40 Abundance. Drawing (black pencil, pen and watercolour, touched with white on reddish prepared paper), 25.3 × 31.7 cm. London, British Museum. The attribution to Botticelli by Ulmann is fully accepted. Can be dated after his stay in Rome, about 1482.

41 Pallas and the Centaur. Canvas, 148 × 207 cm. Florence, Uffizi. Discovered by Ridolfi in a corridor of the Palazzo Pitti, and removed to the Uffizi in 1922. It belonged with the *Spring* to Lorenzo di Pierfrancesco, and was later inherited by Giovanni delle Bande Nere. The allegorical theme has been interpreted in various ways: Ridolfi sees in it the victory of Lorenzo the Magnificent (Pallas representing wisdom) over the court of Naples (the Centaur), and dates it around 1480, immediately after Lorenzo's return from

Naples; Steinmann believes it to symbolize the supremacy of the Medici over the Pazzi; Frothingham, the political balance of power maintained by Lorenzo; Wittkower (very plausibly) the union of wisdom and instinct in the person of Lorenzo, whose device (three diamond rings) is embroidered on Pallas' dress. Perhaps the most acceptable explanation of all is by Gombrich, who traces its meaning to Ficino, whose philosophy was an inspiration for the *Spring*: according to this view the Centaur represents both the sensual side of man (the animal part), and his reason (the human part), subdued by wisdom (Minerva). Berenson agrees with Ridolfi and Yashiro on the date 1480; both Horne and L. Venturi date it 1488, (supposing it to refer to the alliance between Lorenzo and Innocent VIII formed in 1487), while Bode suggests the year 1485, on which Mesnil and Bettini agree. The most reliable date is probably 1482-3, given by A. Venturi, Van Marle, Gamba and Salvini.

42 Lorenzo Tornabuoni Presented to the Seven Liberal Arts. Detached fresco, 269×227 cm. Paris, Louvre. This fresco, with the one below (*pl. 43*), was originally a loggia decoration for a villa belonging to Tornabuoni, near Careggi, later bought by the Lemmi family. The attribution to Botticelli, now universally accepted, stems from Cavalcaselle. The young man in the fresco has been identified as Lorenzo Tornabuoni, who was executed in 1497 after taking part in a plot to secure the return of Piero dei Medici. The girl in the companion fresco is believed to be Giovanna degli Albizi. The identification of Tornabuoni is probably correct, but the girl's identity seems doubtful; the coat of arms near the girl is not that of the Albizi family, while the girl's features differ from those in Ghirlandaio's portrait of her in his *Visitation* in Santa Maria Novella, and in that of the medal by Nicolò Fiorentino. As the Albizi coat of arms has been added in tempera to the first fresco, Salvini reasonably concludes 'this addition was painted at the time of the wedding in 1486, so that both frescoes, originally painted for another occasion, would be associated with the Tornabuoni-Albizi marriage'. Hence the necessity to date this work before 1486. Both frescoes are also in the style of that period.

43 Venus Followed by Graces Offers Gifts to a Girl. Detached fresco, 284 × 212 cm. Paris, Louvre.

44 Venus Followed by Graces Offers Gifts to a Girl. Detail: the Graces.

45 Venus Followed by Graces Offers Gifts to a Girl. Detail of the girl.

46 Second Panel of the Story of Nastagio degli Onesti. Panel, 112×84 cm. Madrid, Prado. Detail. This panel and its companion (*pl. 47*) belong to a group of four which illustrate a tale from Boccaccio. Attributed to Botticelli by Vasari. According to recent critics the design is by Botticelli, but the work was executed by studio assistants. The presence of the coats of arms of the Pucci and Bini families has led Horne to assume that the panels were executed in 1483 for the wedding of Giannozzo Pucci and Lucrezia Bini.

47 Third Panel of the Story of Nastagio degli Onesti. Panel, 112 × 84 cm. Prado, Madrid. Detail.

48 Madonna of the Magnificat. Panel, tondo, diameter 118 cm. Florence, Uffizi. Much repainted, mostly in the faces of the Virgin and Child. Considered an early work by Cavalcaselle, it has since been variously dated by modern critics: Ulmann, Horne, A. Venturi, Gamba, Argan and Salvini suggest a date about 1482, Yashiro and Van Marle agree on 1481, before the artist's journey to Rome, while Bode, followed by Schmarsow, Venturi and Bettini, favours the year 1485.

49 Madonna of the Magnificat. Detail of the Virgin.

50 Madonna and Child. Panel, 39.5×58 cm. Milan, Museo Poldi Pezzoli. It is universally acknowledged as an authentic work, and is generally agreed to have been painted more or less at the same time as the *Madonna of the Magnificat.*

51 Madonna and Child. Detail of the Child (see *pl. 51*).

52 Venus and Mars. Panel, 173.5×69 cm. London, National Gallery. Ulmann, followed by most critics, dates it around 1485-6, immediately after the *Birth of Venus*, while Bode and Van Marle believe it was painted in 1476-8; Schmarsow, with whom Argan agrees, dates it back to 1475. Salvini maintains it was painted shortly before the *Birth of Venus*, in 1483. Here again, we turn to Gombrich for the interpretation of the subject as an idea derived from Ficino (the influence of Venus, seen as *humanitas*, on Mars the symbol of war).

53 Birth of Venus. Detail: Venus (see *pl. 55*).

54 Birth of Venus. Detail of Hour (see *pl. 55*).

55 Birth of Venus. Canvas, 278.5×172.5 cm. Florence, Uffizi. Its presence in the Villa del Castello suggests that it was painted for Lorenzo di Pierfrancesco. Later it became the property of Giovanni delle Bande Nere and finally of Cosimo I. Its date is a matter of some controversy: Bode suggests 1478; Ulmann, followed by Horne, A. Venturi, Gamba, L. Venturi, Bettini and Argan, thinks it was painted in 1485-6; Yashiro in 1487, Van Marle in 1481-2, Salvini in 1484. The subject of the painting is evidently inspired by the Homeric hymn to Venus, by the stanzas of Poliziano, and partly by Ovid. Wickhoff thought it represented the arrival of Venus in Sicily, as narrated in the *Pervigilium Veneris.* Here too, the most reliable analysis is by Gombrich, who mentions Ficino's and Pico della Mirandola's interpretations of the Birth of Venus as narrated by Hesiod (the goddess was generated from the testicles of Uranus, castrated by Chronos and cast into the sea). This story was interpreted as the birth of Beauty from the union of Idea and Matter.

56 Madonna of the Pomegranate. Panel, tondo, diameter 143.5 cm. Florence, Uffizi. Horne (followed by A. Venturi, Gamba, Bettini and Salvini) believes that this tondo should be identified with one which Botticelli painted in 1487 for the court-room of the Magistrato dei Massai in the Palazzo Vecchio. This hypothesis seems to be supported by the frame, decorated with a frieze of lilies. But this identification and dating of the tondo is not shared by Ulmann (who suggests a date previous to 1480), Bode, Schmarsow, Yashiro, L. Venturi (*c.* 1482), Berenson, Mesnil or Van Marle.

57 Madonna of the Pomegranate. Detail of the Virgin.

58 San Barnaba Altarpiece. Panel, 280 × 268 cm. Florence, Uffizi. Painted for the convent of San Barnaba, it was moved to the Accademia when the convent was closed, and later to the Uffizi. It represents the Madonna and Child on a throne with four angels and Saints Catherine of Alexandria, Augustine, Barnabas, John the Baptist, Ignatius and Michael the Archangel. Mentioned in early sources (Albertini, Antonio Bini, Vasari). Dates vary from 1480 to 1494. Il was probably painted as Salvini suggests, c. 1488. Ulmann dates it 1480, Horne, Bode, Schmarsow, Yashiro, L. and A. Venturi in 1482-3; Gamba, Bettini and Argan suggest it was begun 1487 and completed some years later.

59 San Barnaba Altarpiece. Detail of St John the Baptist, St Ignatius and St Michael the Archangel.

60· Annunciation. Panel, 156 × 150 cm. Florence, Uffizi. Cited by Vasari as an authentic work and located by him in the church of Santa Maria Maddalena dei Pazzi. Documents found by Milanesi suggest that the panel was executed between 1489 and 1490. Its authenticity is acknowledged by Ulmann, Bode, A. and L. Venturi, Mesnil and Salvini; it is attributed to Sandro's studio by Morelli, Yashiro, Van Marle, Berenson, Gamba and Bettini.

61 Annunciation. Detail of landscape.

62 Madonna and Child with Young St John. Panel, 73.5 × 89.5 cm. Dresden, Gemäldegalerie. Accepted as Botticelli's unaided work by some critics (Morelli, Gamba and Salvini). Ulmann, A. Venturi, Berenson and Mesnil among others consider it a studio work, painted towards the end of 1490.

63 Annunciation. Panel, 36×24 cm. New York, Lehman Collection. Acknowledged as Botticelli's work by Ulmann, Bode, Schmarsow, Van Marle, Yashiro, L. Venturi, Gamba, Salvini; dates vary from

1474 to after 1500. Attributed to the school of Botticelli by Morelli, Horne and A. Venturi. I agree with Bode, who dates this predella panel between 1485 and 1490.

64 St Augustine in his Cell. Panel, 27 × 41 cm. Florence, Uffizi. Morelli's attribution is accepted, though dates vary from about 1490 (Ulmann, Horne, Bode, Van Marle and Salvini) to 1495 (A. Venturi, Gamba) and 1500 (Yashiro, Bettini).

65 Nativity. Pen and watercolour touched with white on prepared paper, 26 × 16 cm. Florence, Uffizi. Unanimously attributed to Sandro, and dated 1491 (Yashiro).

66 Lamentation. Panel, 207 × 110 cm. Munich, Alte Pinakothek. Formerly in the church of San Paolino, bought in 1815 for King Ludwig of Bavaria. Acknowledged as autograph by Cavalcaselle, Ulmann, Morelli, Bode, Schmarsow, A. and L. Venturi, Gamba, Mesnil, Bettini, Argan and Salvini, as a workshop painting by Berenson, Horne, Van Marle. Date of execution c. 1490.

67 Lamentation. Panel, 71 × 107 cm. Milan, Museo Poldi Pezzoli. Some critics think this is the panel mentioned by Vasari in Santa Maria Maggiore (identified by others with the Munich *Lamentation, pl. 66*). Other believe both *Lamentations* are versions of the *Pietà* in Santa Maria Maggiore (Horne). The ascription to Botticelli is favoured by Ulmann, Bode, Schmarsow, Van Marle, Gamba, Bettini, Argan and Salvini. May be dated, like the Munich *Lamentation,* to the last decade of the fifteenth century.

68 Drawing for Canto XXXIII of Dante's Purgatorio. 32 × 47 cm. Formerly in Berlin, Kupferstichkabinett. Botticelli illustrated the *Commedia* for Lorenzo di Pierfrancesco (Anonimo Gaddiano). These drawings have been identified as those found in a codex in the Hamilton Library, which was bought in Paris in 1803, then transferred in its entirety to the Berlin Museum in 1882. Some of the missing pages of the Hamilton codex were found in a miscellaneous one in the Vatican. Each folio contained one Canto set out in four columns on the recto, and a drawing illustrating the following Canto on the verso. These lead and silverpoint drawings were meant to be coloured. The Vatican Library owns the plan of the *Inferno,* which has an illustration for Canto I of the *Inferno* on the back, and also drawings for Cantos IX, X, XII, XIII, XV, XVI; while in Berlin, prior to the second world war, drawings existed for Canto VIII and XVII-XXXIV of the *Inferno* as well as all the *Purgatorio* and *Paradiso* drawings, except XXX and XXXIII of the *Paradiso.* Unfortunately, nearly all the Berlin sheets were dispersed during the war. Only three drawings (*Inferno* XXIX and XXXI, and *Purgatorio* III) are now to be found in the Staatliche Museen in Berlin. All are universally accepted as authentic; the date must be related to the political events, between 1490-6, affecting the career of Lorenzo di Pierfrancesco, by whom these works were commissioned.

69 Drawing for Canto XXIX of the Paradiso. 32 × 47 cm. Formerly in Berlin, Kupferstichkabinett.

70 Calumny. Panel, 91 × 62 cm. Florence, Galleria degli Uffizi. Mentioned by Vasari as being in the house of Fabio Segni. The subject is derived from a famous painting by Apelles, described in Lucian's *De Calumnia*, which Botticelli presumably read in a Latin translation either by Guarino Veronese or Fontio (1472), or else in the Florentine edition of 1496. Lucian's description is also paraphrased by Alberti (*De Pictura*, 1434). The allegory represents a youth carried away by Calumny, who is accompanied by Deceit and Fraud, and brought into the presence of King Midas, beside whom stand Ignorance and Suspicion. Near Calumny stands Penitence, an old woman, and, on the left side of the painting, a naked girl represents Truth. The date of this work is generally placed in the last decade of the century.

71 Calumny. Detail: Truth.

72 Calumny. Detail: Penitence.

73 Story of Virginia. Panel, 165 × 86 cm. Bergamo, Accademia Carrara. Ascribed to Botticelli by Morelli. It has been identified as one of the panel paintings mentioned by Vasari, and located by him in Giovanni Vespucci's house. All critics agree on the ascription and dating of the work in the last decade of the century.

74 Mystic Nativity. Canvas, 75 × 108.5 cm. London, National Gallery. It has been in the National Gallery since 1878. It was brought to England from Rome at the end of the eighteenth century, and found its way into various English collections. In the upper part of the painting there is a Greek epigraph which can be translated as follows: 'I Sandro painted this picture at the end of year 1500 [i.e. early in 1501] in the troubles of Italy in the mid-time after the time according to the 11th chapter of St John in the second woe of the Apocalypse in the loosing of the devil for three and a half years then he will be chained in the 12th chapter and we shall see clearly ... as in this picture.' It is commonly accepted that this canvas represents the prophesy of Liberation (the birth of Christ as a triumph of the divine world) from the reign of the Antichrist, who manifested himself through the disorders in Italy to which this inscription refers, and in the death of Savonarola.

1

2

3

4

5

6

7

9

11

12

13

14

15

16

17

18

20

21

–22

23

24

25

28 – 29

30

32

33

35

37→

36

39

40

42

43

–44

45

47

49 →

48

50

51

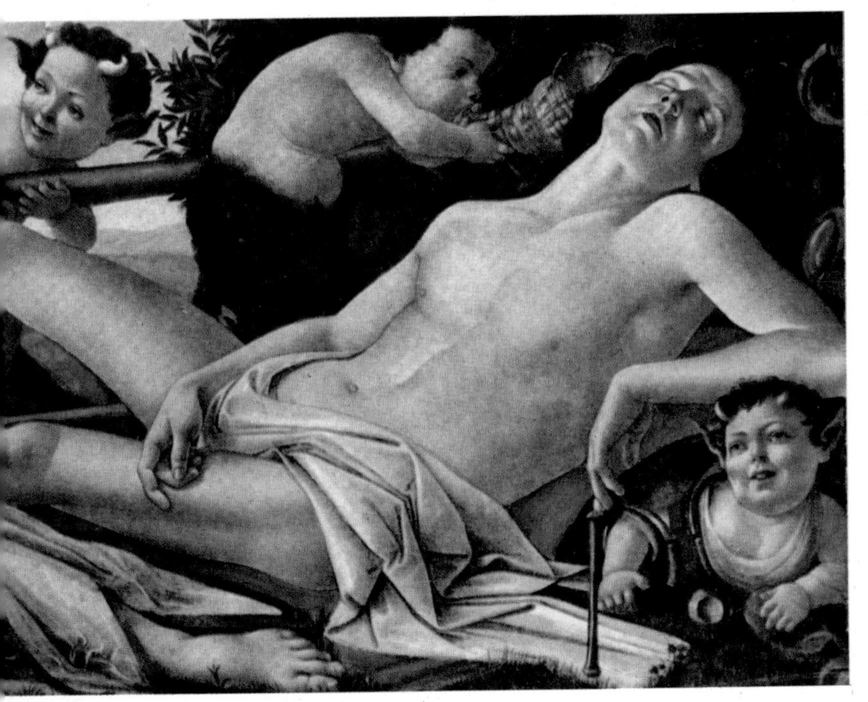

57

58

60

61

62

63

64

65

66

67

69

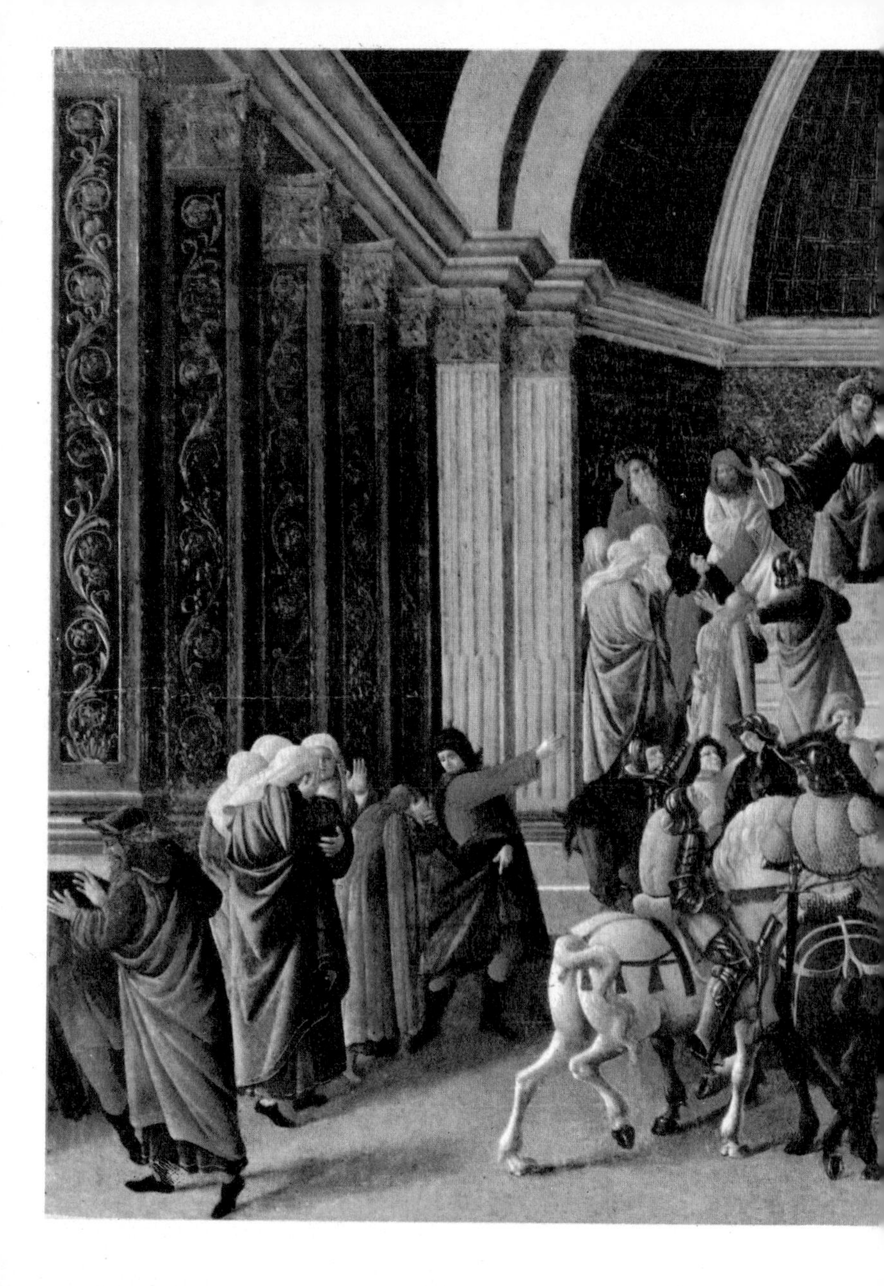